Cascading Cardigan Vest
Lace Crochet Pattern
A seamless lace crochet halter top pattern
by
Kristen Stein

ISBN: 9781081122430
Imprint: Independently Published

Contents

Motif Lace Crochet

Introduction

I love crocheting garments using lace-inspired motifs. They are a quick and relatively easy way to create crocheted fabric that can be made into beautiful, lacy, and flexible garments or accessories. Motif crochet uses repeated patterns to create individual motifs that are seamlessly joined together to create an overall crocheted fabric. The designer then creates a garment using the crocheted fabric in much the same way that one would sew a pattern using regular yards of fabric.

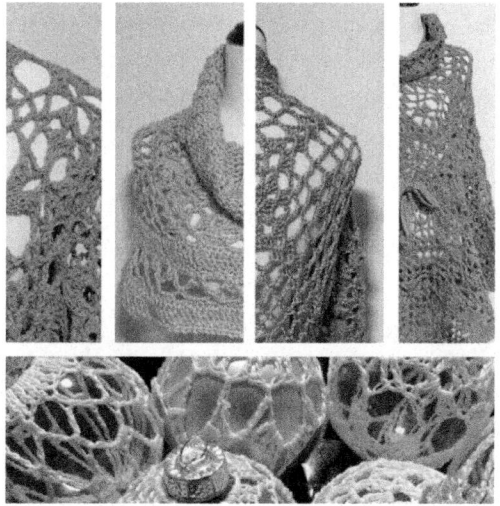

Photo 1: A few of my other patterns using Motif Lace Crochet.

What makes motif crochet fun and flexible is that it is usually accomplished with relatively simple repeated rounds. This breaks up the monotony of row by row stitches and allows the designer greater control over the shape of the final crocheted fabric or garment. By joining the motifs to one another during the final round, the designer is able to create a seamless crocheted fabric that is loose, flexible and drapes beautifully across the body.

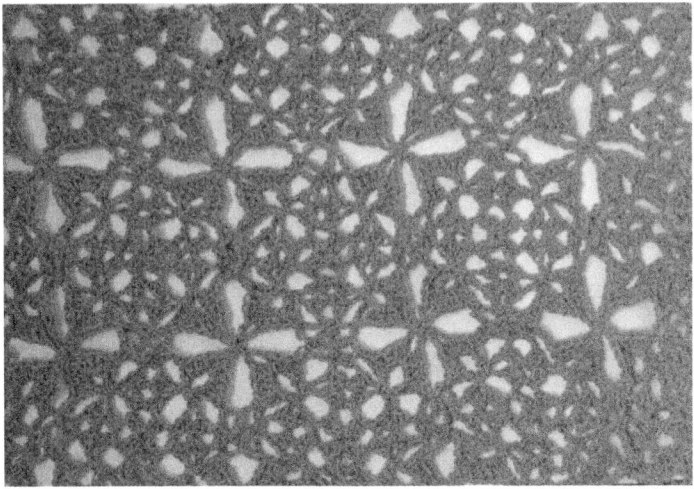

Photo 2: Example of Motif Crochet Panel

The fabric created with motifs usually has significant stretch given the lacy open areas created by the joining stitches. This additional stretch is great because it allows the garment to adapt well to many different body shapes and sizes. The overall size of the garment will be determined after stretching and blocking the garment at the end of the creation process. By properly blocking the garment at the end of the crocheting process, you'll be able to create a garment with the ideal dimensions for your body size and shape.

Motif crocheted fabric can also be modified easily in the sense that you can increase or decrease sizes by simply changing the hook size, or modifying the number of rounds of each motif. This way, you can easily turn a top into a tunic, a scarf into a wrap, or a short-sleeve to a long-sleeve by simply adding additional motifs.

The fabric crocheted with motifs is also forgiving. It is difficult to see errors made in the stitches because the design is flexible, open and the stitches move in many directions. Unlike repeated rows, it is visually more difficult to see a skipped or dropped stitch. This is extremely useful as you begin to make your garment because you don't have to be bothered by small mistakes that you might have made. They are often absorbed into the lacework and visually missed by anyone viewing the completed project.

Another wonderful feature of a lace motif garment is that there are rarely any shoulder or side seams. In most cases, the garment is created by joining motifs during their final rounds. This makes it convenient if you accidentally wear the garment 'inside out' as there are no seams to see. But, a possible drawback from this approach is that there are two yarn tails to each motif that must be woven in as you go, or woven in at the end of each motif connection. You will want to leave the ends long enough to weave them into the garment. That way, you won't have a bunch of yarn ends poking out of the final garment. I try to incorporate the yarn ends into each new motif as I go. That way, I don't have to hunt for all of them at the end of the final project.

The beauty of the crocheted motif fabric is not only in the design of the motif itself, but also in the way in which the motifs join together. The design created from the joining stitches can sometimes be just as intricate as the details within the actual motif. You'll notice this when you block the garment and actually get to wear the finished piece. The contrast between the light and dark areas created by the stitches makes for a visually appealing garment that looks beautiful from all angles.

In this pattern, the motifs are not difficult to crochet. They use very straightforward stitches. The end result, however, looks like an intricate series of stitches yielding a romantic lace-inspired cascading cardigan vest that looks complicated to make. Yet, it truly is not difficult to replicate. The motifs are actually quite simple once you start creating them. The intricate stitch work and lace-inspired look comes from how the motifs are designed and connected to one another during each final round of the motif pattern.

Pattern Notes

When creating my garment designs, I usually create my own patterned paper and then draw out my designs connecting shapes as I go. I decide what geometric shapes work best for the garment that I am making. I found that certain shapes fit better together and provide a visually appealing final product. Given how many lines and grids I was drawing by hand, I decided to create patterned paper to aid in my design process. I recently added a few of these design notebooks to my Amazon Author page. These books are filled with lined pages and patterned pages of (squares, hexagons and other geometric shapes.) These patterned notebooks should prove useful to fashion designers especially those that knit, crochet, sew or quilt. A few of the design books are shown in the next image. Additional information about these sketch & design books are available in the back of the book.

Additional sketch and design
books are also available.
Visit my Amazon author page or
blog for more information.

Photo 3: New line of designer's notebooks and sketchbooks to aid in the design process.

The pattern for my "Cascading Cardigan Vest" consists of 13 motifs: 6 Square Motifs and 7 Pentagonal Motifs. These motifs will be connected to one another in a certain order as you crochet thereby creating a beautiful seamless garment. (See Figure 1.) The motifs will join with one another by connecting certain sides together with 'joining stitches' as we progress through the pattern. This will be explained in more detail when we get to the section called "The Joining Round".

The motif patterns I created result in motifs that measure approximately 10" wide along one edge. Due to its design, the motif will have significant ability to stretch. We will stretch the item to fit (if needed) when we get to the blocking stage at the end of the pattern. The extra stretch of the motif will provide incredible comfort and a great fit for a variety of body shapes and sizes.

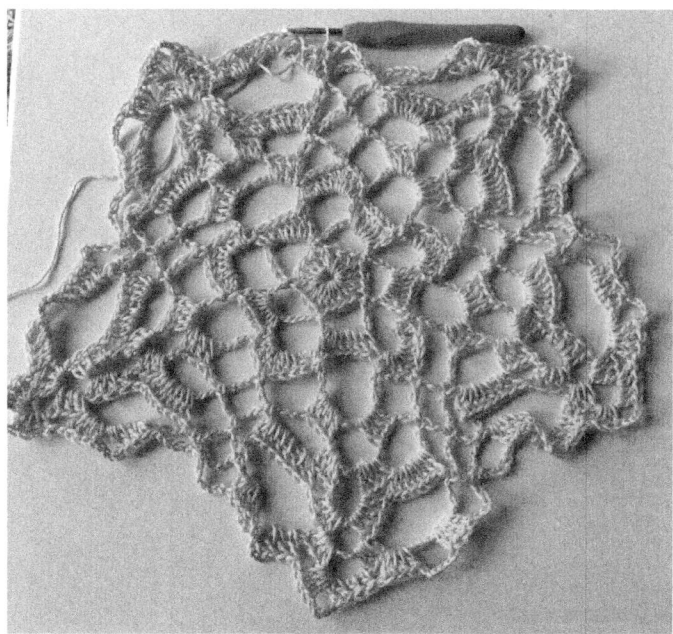

Photo 4: One Complete Pentagonal Motif

The pattern is created to fit most people as it is a "one-size-fits most" pattern. You can decrease the hook size to make smaller motifs suitable for a more petite figure. For larger sizes, you can increase the hook size. Please keep in mind, that the motifs are stretchy, so you can easily block the garment at the end if you want to stretch the piece to fit larger. These size adjustments will be discussed in more detail when we get to the actual pattern.

Figure 1: Order of Motifs and Side Joins

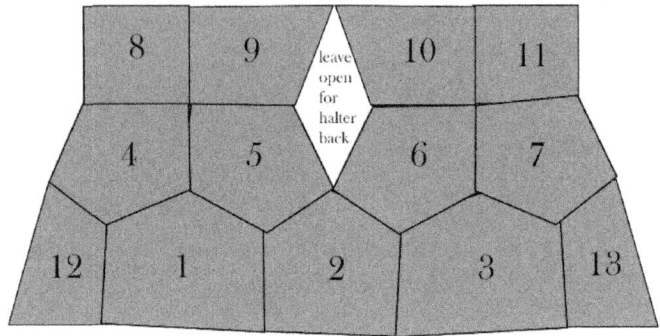

Begin with Motif 1 and join motif edges as you go according to diagram above.
Motifs 1-7 are pentagonal motifs.
Motifs 8-13 are square motifs.
One side edge of Motifs 5, 6, 9 & 10 are left unjoined to create halter back opening.

Figure 1: Order of Motifs and Side Joins

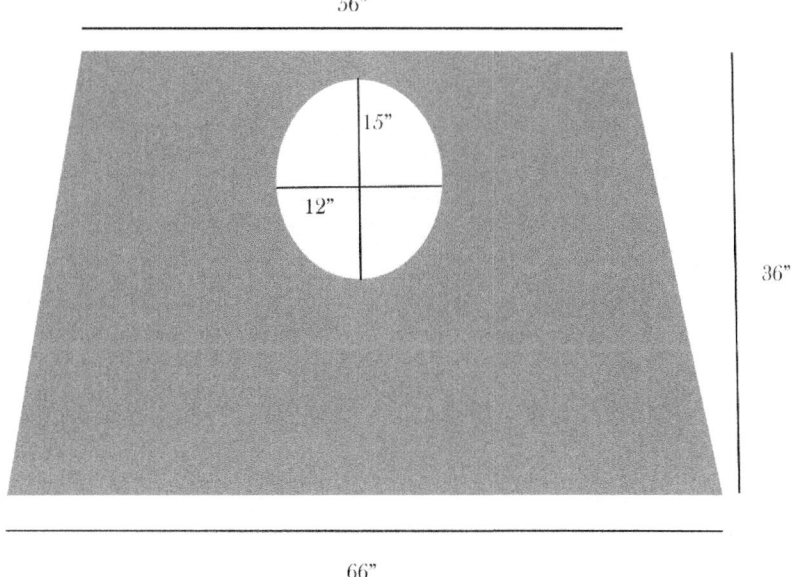

Figure 2: Approximate Garment Dimensions (laid flat after blocking)

Drape of garment when viewed from the back.

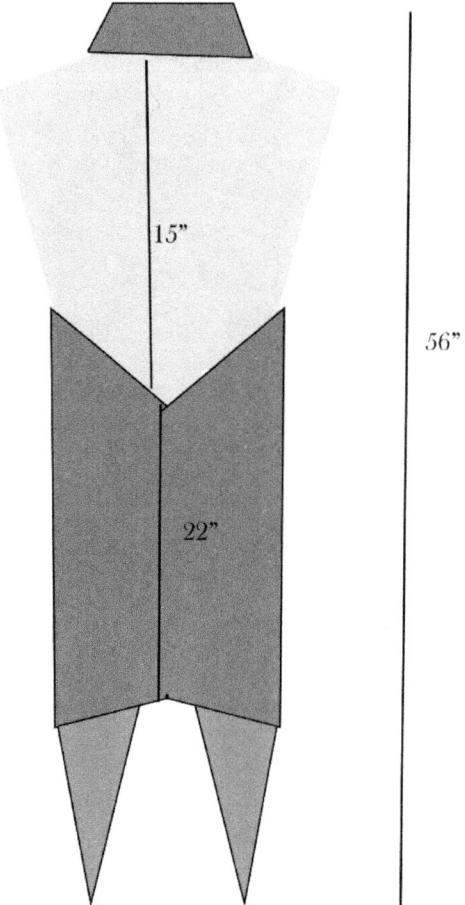

Figure 3: *Approximate drape of garment when viewed from the back.*

Notes on the "Joining Round"

The garment is created "seamlessly as-you-go" in the sense that each motif is joined to an existing motif as you crochet. You will start with Motif 1 and continue to Motif 13 joining motifs according to Figure 1. Each motif is crocheted in 9 rounds. The first 8 rounds are the "preliminary rounds". Round 9 is the "final round". Each motif is "joined" to previous motifs during the motif's final round. The final round is also called the "joining round". In this pattern only Motif 1 will be made from start to finish with a final round that doesn't join to another motif.

Referring back to Figure 1, Motif 1 is our starting motif. Each additional motif (2-13) will be made with the preliminary rounds and then 'joined' to existing motifs during its final "joining" round. The joins are created with chain stitches. You will accomplish the 'join' by breaking up the designated chain stitch halfway through its creation. For instance, in this pattern, the joining chain spaces are created as either a chain 6 loop along the sides or a chain 4 loop in the corners. We create the "join" during the final round by creating half the number of chain stitches and then joining with a slip stitch to the corresponding corner or side on a previously-made motif. We then complete the chain 4 or the chain 6 to 'complete the chain' and continue to work the final round on the motif we are making. This joining process will feel like a 'zig-zag' movement between the motif on whose final round you are working and a previously completed motif that you are seamlessly joining into the crocheted garment. We join as we go in order to allow the garment and crocheted fabric to take shape. For this garment, we will join motifs to one another in the order illustrated by Figure 1. (**Designer note**: When you begin making the garment, you might want to print out a copy of Figure 1 so that you can use it for quick reference. You might also want to have stitch markers on hand to clip the top of the garment, or the most recently made motif, so that you can easily keep track of the pattern as the garment grows in size.)

Here are a few additional notes to further illustrate the joining process. This will be discussed in more detail when we get to the actual pattern.

Looking back at Figure 1, you see that Motif 1 is crocheted as one complete motif using the patterns rounds 1-9. You'll fasten off and weave in the yarn ends. Then, you will start Motif 2 and complete rounds 1-8. Then, you'll start the final round 9 which will consist of one side that will be joined along two consecutive corners to the existing Motif 1. Once the shared edge is 'joined', you'll continue to finish the remaining sides of Motif 2 without joining them to another motif. You'll fasten off Motif 2. Weave in ends and then move onto Motif 3. We will discuss each of the Motif joins in greater detail when we move onto the actual pattern.

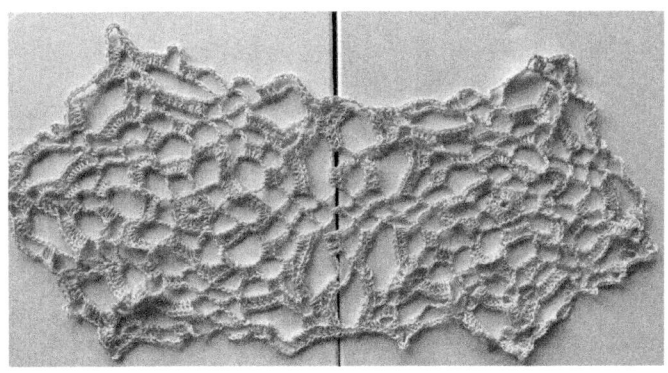

Photo 5: Motif 1 joined to Motif 2 along one edge between consecutive corners..

You will then complete the crocheted 'fabric' by joining motifs up to Motif 13 as given by Figure 1.

Special "Joining Rounds"

There are a few motifs that have "special joining rounds". We want to leave an opening in the back to create the halter-top back. We will accomplish this by leaving the side edges of Motifs 5, 6, 9 & 10 unjoined during the joining process. By leaving these edges unjoined, we will create a nice round opening that is perfect for the open back of the cascading cardigan.

Final pattern notes: Once you successfully join Motif 13, the motif portion of the pattern will be complete, we will then move onto crocheting the trim for the back-opening and perimeter edging.

You will then block the garment and stretch to the desired dimensions or use the dimensions that I provide in the pattern.

Photo 6: The completed garment

Photo 7: The finished garment (back view).

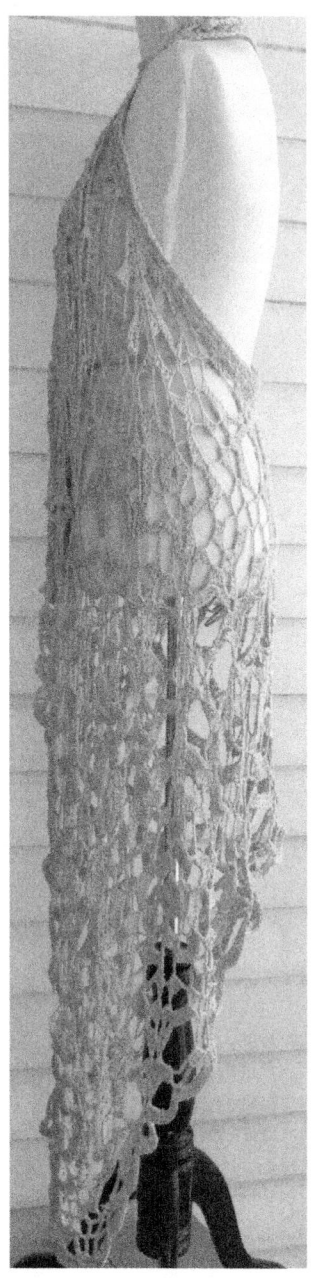

Photo 8: Completed Garment (Side View)

Photo 9: Garment Back Closeup.

Cascading Cardigan Vest Lace Crochet Pattern

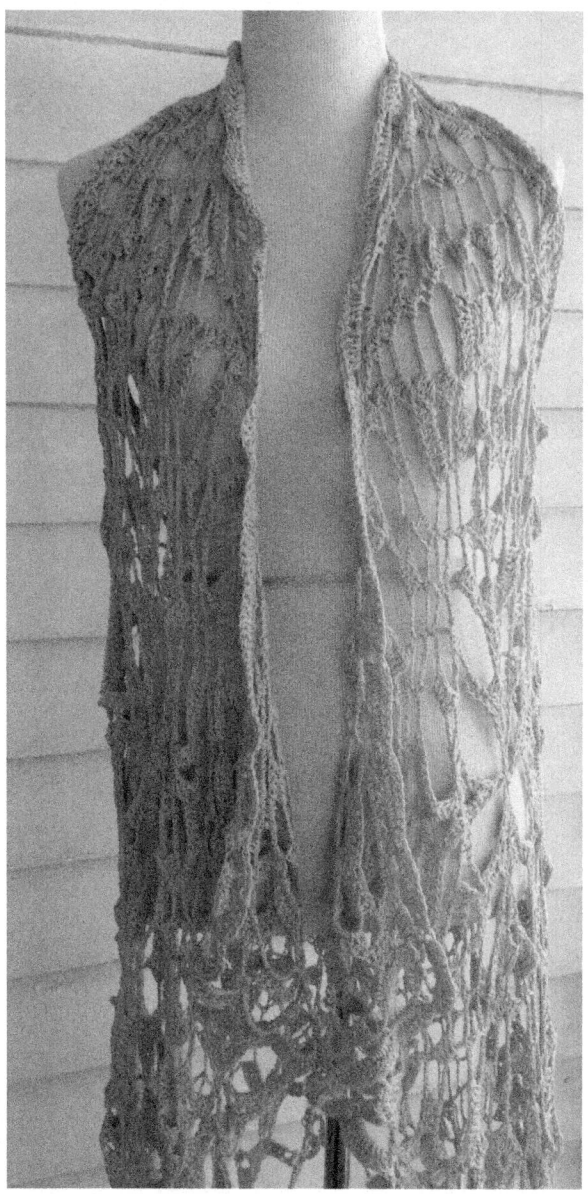

Photo 10: Garment front closeup.

Stitches Used & Abbreviations

(A **stitch glossary** is provided at the end of the pattern. Note that the pattern might not use every stitch listed here.)

Chain (ch)

Double-Crochet (dc)

Half-Double-Crochet (hdc)

Picot (p)

Single-Crochet (sc)

Slip Stitch (sl st)

Treble-Crochet (tr)

Treble-Crochet Together (trtog) (Specifically tr2tog & tr3tog)

Other Abbreviations you might see in this pattern:

Pattern (Pat)

Repeat (Rep)

Right-Side (RS)

Round (Rd)

Skip (sk)

Space (sp)

Wrong Side (WS)

Yarn Over (YO)

Pattern

Materials used:

Yarn
DK, #3 weight

As shown: 8 skeins of Cascade Yarns Ultra Pima Fine in Peach Pearl #3810. 100% Pima Cotton. Each skein is 136.7 yards (125m) / 1.75 oz (50g).

Hook
Crochet Hook 5.0mm. or size needed to obtain gauge.

Gauge
The Motif should measure approximately 4.5" after Round 4 and 8" after Round 7. After the final Round 9, one edge of the Motif should measure about 10" wide. (unstretched)

Finished Size
Laid flat after blocking, the garment, as shown, measures approximately 56" across at the top, 66" across at the bottom, 36" from top to bottom and the back-opening is about 12" by 15".

The overall drape of the garment when worn is about 56" from neck to longest point in front. The drape in the back is about 22" and the back-opening is about 15"

The garment has considerable give as it is an open crochet, and the motifs have significant stretch, but if you want to adjust this for a fuller figure, you can increase the hook size to a 5.5mm or 6.0mm hook to make larger motifs or add an additional round to the motifs. For a shorter, or tighter garment, you can decrease the hook size to a 4.0-4.5mm hook.

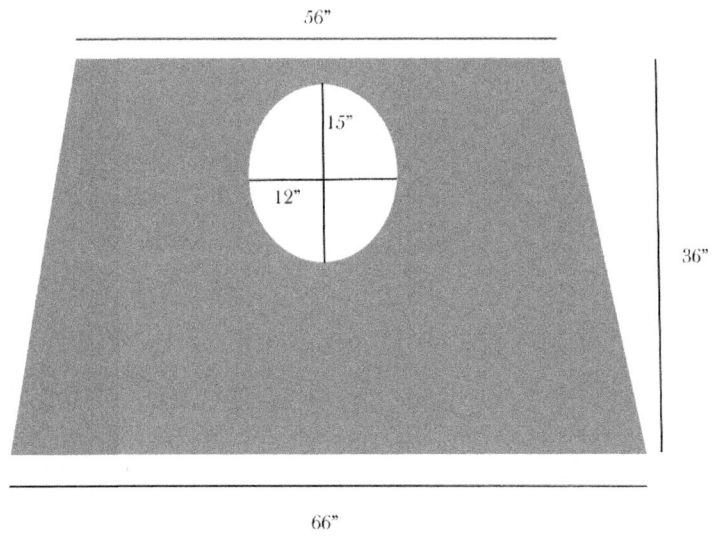

Photo 11: Approximate Garment Measurements (laid flat). After blocking.

28

Drape of garment when viewed from the back.

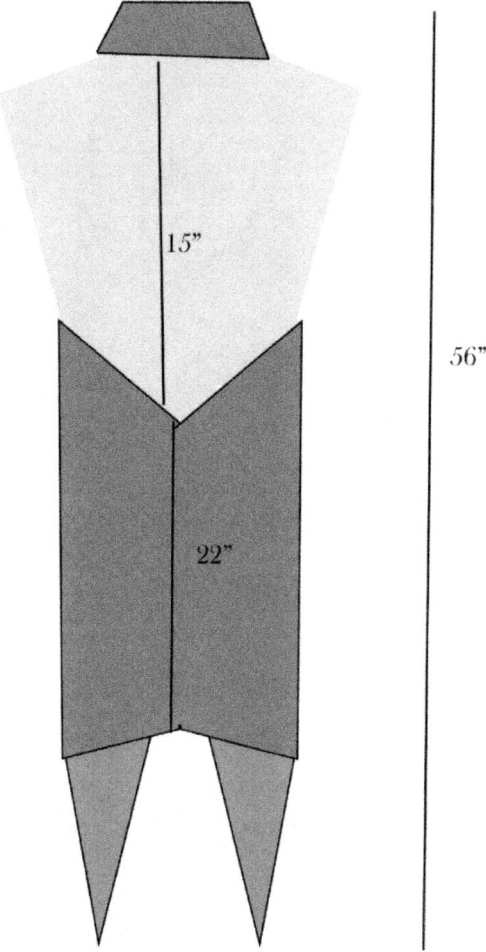

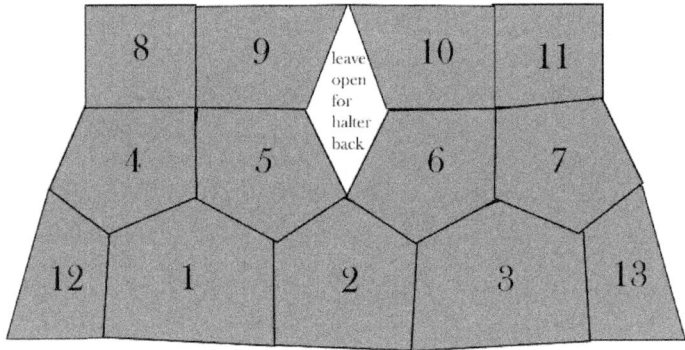

Begin with Motif 1 and join motif edges as you go according to diagram above.
Motifs 1-7 are pentagonal motifs.
Motifs 8-13 are square motifs.
One side edge of Motifs 5, 6, 9 & 10 are left unjoined to create halter back opening.

Figure 1: Order of Motifs and Side Joins

Figure 1 is repeated here for easy viewing while reading the pattern. When you begin making the garment, you might want to print out a copy of Figure 1 so that you can use it for quick reference.

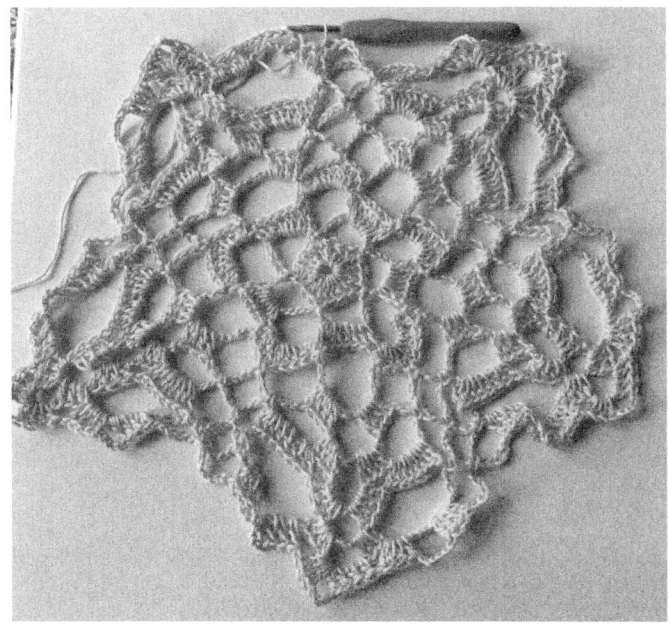

Photo 12: The completed Pentagon Motif.

The Motif Pattern

(Refer back to Figure 1 to join the motifs as you go. You'll need to connect the motifs on certain sides as you complete the final round of each motif. See my pattern notes at the beginning of this book for a better understanding of how to join the motifs as you proceed. The joining process will also be discussed in more detail as we progress through the pattern.)

The Pentagon Motif Pattern

Ch5. Slip stitch in first stitch of starting chain to form a ring.

Round 1 (Rd 1): ch3 (acts as 1st dc); 19dc in ring. Slip stitch to top of opening ch3 to end the round.

End with 20 dc.

Photo 13: Pentagon Motif after Round 1.

Rd 2: *ch9; skip 3dc; slip stitch into next dc **; repeat from * to ** around. Slip stitch into 1st ch9 space to end the round.

End with 5 ch9 loops.

Photo 14: Motif after Round 2.

Rd 3: (ch3,7dc) in opening ch9 space; ch9; *8dc in next ch9 space; ch9 **; repeat from * to ** around. Slip stitch in top of opening ch3 to end the round.

End with 5 ch9 spaces and 5 8dc clusters. Motif measures approximately 3.5" across one edge

Photo 15: The pentagon motif after Round 3.

Rd4: ch15; *skip 6dc; slip stitch in next dc; 8dc in next ch9 space***; slip stitch in first dc; ch15**; repeat from * to ** around. On final repeat, end at *** and slip stitch into first ch15 space to end the round.

End with 5 ch15 loops and 5 8dc clusters.

Check your gauge. The motif should measure approximately 4.5" across one edge.

Photo 16:The motif after Round 4.

Rd 5:. (ch3 (acts as first dc), 3dc, ch9, 4dc) in opening ch15 space; *ch6; skip 3dc; sc in next dc; ch6***; (4dc, ch9, 4dc) in next ch15 space**; repeat from * to ** around. On final repeat, end at *** and instead of a ch6, create a ch3 and dc into the top of the starting ch3 to end the round. The combination of a (ch3 + dc) will mimic the final ch6, but will allow us to end in the center of the space which is a better starting position for the next round.

End with 10 ch6 spaces and 5 ch9 spaces.

Photo 17: The motif after Round 5.

Rd6: sc in opening ch6 space; ch6; *(4dc, ch9, 4dc) in next ch9 space; ch6; sc in next ch6 space; ch6***; sc in next ch6 space; ch6**; repeat from * to ** around. On final repeat, end at *** and slip stitch to starting sc to end the round.

End with 15 ch6 spaces and 5 ch9 spaces available for the next round.

Motif should measure approximately 7" across one edge.

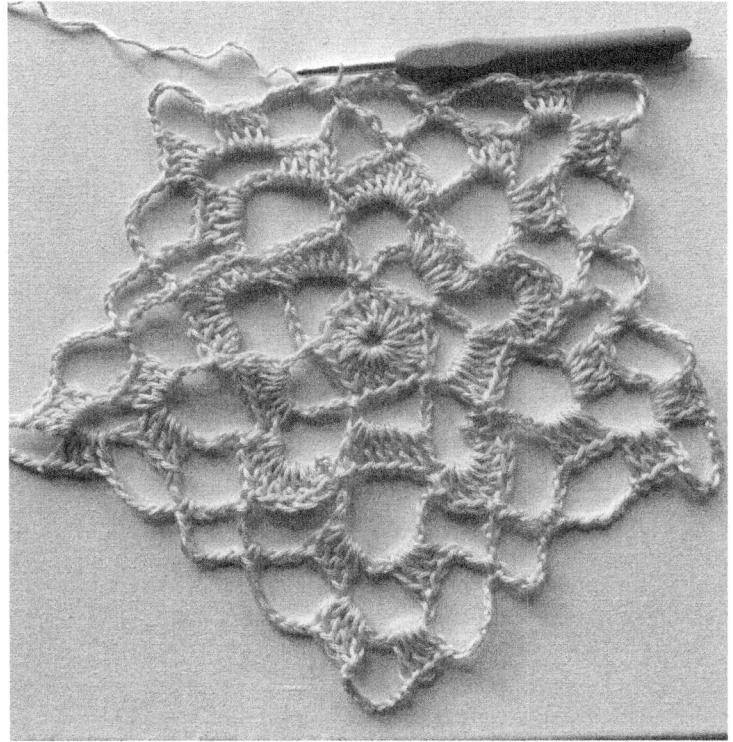

Photo 18: The motif after Round 6.

Beginning with Round 7, we will have a more defined corner "ch4 space".

Rd 7: Slip stitch into the next ch6 space (it should be the ch6 space before the 4dc corner cluster); (ch3,7dc) in same ch6 space; *(4dc, ch4, 4dc) in next ch9 space; 8dc in next ch6 space; ch6; sc in next ch6 space; ch6***; 8dc in next ch6 space**; repeat from * to ** around. On final repeat, end at ***, but instead of a ch6 create a ch3 and dc into top of the starting ch3 to end the round. This combination of (ch3+dc) allows us to start the next round in the center of the final space.

End with 10 ch6 side spaces and 5 corner ch4 spaces. Motif should measure approximately 8" across one edge.

Photo 19: Motif after Round 7. Approximately 8" across one edge.

Rd 8: sc in opening ch6 space; *ch12; (4dc, ch4, 4dc) in corner ch4 space; ch12; sc in ch6 space; ch6; sc in next ch6 space**; repeat from * to ** around. Slip stitch to starting sc to end the round.

End with 10 ch12 spaces, 5 ch 6 spaces and 5 ch4 corner spaces.

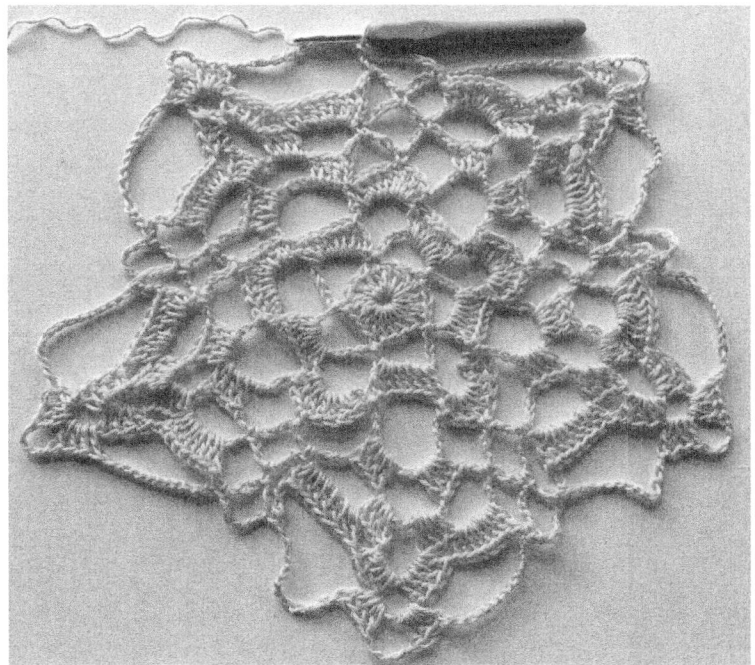

Photo 20: Motif after Round 8.

Rd 9: (Final "Joining" Rd) Remember: For Motif 1 do the complete Round 9 without joining to other motifs. For all other motifs at least one side will be a joining edge to join with one or more other motifs that you have already made. Refer to Figure 1 and the Pattern Notes at the beginning of the book to review the joining rounds and the special joins. It is easiest to start joining in the corner **ch4** point. The joining process for all Motifs other than Motif 1 are indicated by the bold typeface below.

Slip stitch into the 1st ch12 space; (ch3,3dc, ch6, 4dc) in same ch12 space; *(4dc, **ch4 or join**, 4dc) in next ch4 corner space; (4dc, **ch6 or join**, 4dc) in next ch12 space; **ch6 or join**; sc in next ch6 space; **ch6 or join*****; (4dc, **ch6 or join**, 4dc) in next ch12 space**; repeat from * to ** around. On final repeat, end at *** and slip stitch to top of starting ch3 to end the round.

Fasten off. Weave in ends.

End with 20 ch6 side spaces and 5 ch4 corner spaces that will be used for joining motifs as we progress through the pattern.

The motif should measure about 10" wide unstretched.

(**Note:** The stitches highlighted in bold identify the stitches that are the joining stitches. Here you will substitute (**ch2, slip stitch to other motif, ch2**) in place of the **ch4** on all loops requiring a ch4 join. You'll substitute (**ch3, slip stitch to other motif, ch3**) in place of the **ch6** on all loops requiring a ch6 join. If you are not joining a side or corner, then do the final round just as you did Motif 1 using a ch4 or ch6 without a joining stitch in the middle. Continue to create the final round joining in the spaces as needed to create the garment according to Figure 1.)

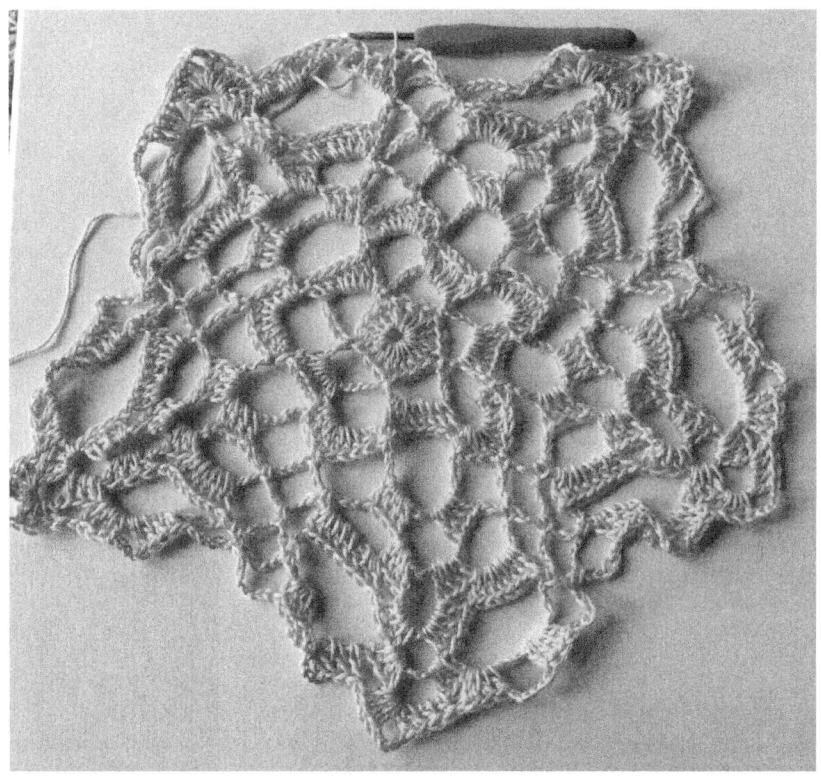

Photo 21: Motif 1 after the Final Round (Rd 9).

Congratulations! Motif 1 is a now complete. The motif should measure approximately 10" unstretched along one side. It will stretch as we proceed through the pattern and when we block the final garment.

Motifs 2-7

Pentagon Motifs 2-7 will begin just like Motif 1. You'll make them the same way through the preliminary rounds 1-8. It's only the final "joining" round that differs. During the "join" you won't create a ch4 or a ch6 in the joining positions. You will instead break these chains in half and slip stitch to the corresponding space on a previously made motif to seamlessly join them together. You'll then complete the ch4 or the ch6 when you return back to the final round of the motif on which you are working. In this way, you will mimic the ch4 or the ch6 spaces, but you are able to seamlessly pick up other motifs as you go. This should feel like a 'zig-zag' movement between the current motif on which you are working and the previously made motifs that you are joining.

For example, here is how you will create Motif 2 and join it to the previously made Motif 1.

Repeat **Rd1-Rd8** of the Pentagon Motif Pattern in the same way you made Motif 1.

When you get to the final round, do the following:

Motif 2's Joining Round (Rd9):

We will begin the join in the first corner of Motif 2 and zig-zag between Motif 2 and Motif 1 to pick up Motif 1 using its side ch6 spaces and its ch4 corner loops.

Let's begin:

Slip stitch into the 1st ch12 space on Motif 2; (ch3, 3dc, ch6, 4dc) in same ch12 space on Motif 2; (4dc, **ch2, slip stitch in first corner ch4 space of Motif 1, ch2**, 4dc) in next ch4 corner space on Motif 2; (4dc, **ch3, slip stitch into first ch6 space on Motif 1, ch3**, 4dc) in next ch12 space on Motif 2 ; **ch3, slip stitch into next ch6 space on Motif 1, ch3**; sc in next ch6 space on Motif 2; **ch3, slip stitch into next ch6 space on Motif 1, ch3**; (4dc, **ch3, slip stitch into next ch6 space on Motif 1, ch3**, 4dc) in next ch12 space on Motif 2; (4dc, **ch2, slip stitch in next corner ch4 space of Motif 1, ch2**, 4dc) in next ch4 corner space of Motif 2.

You have now joined one complete side of Motif 2 to Motif 1 using two consecutive ch4 corners.

Work the remaining edges of Motif 2 just like the final round of Motif 1 without using any joining slip stitches to other motifs. The remaining edges will be completed with regular ch4 and ch6 spaces without the additional joining slip stitch. Fasten off when you get to the end and weave in the ends. Move onto Motif 3.

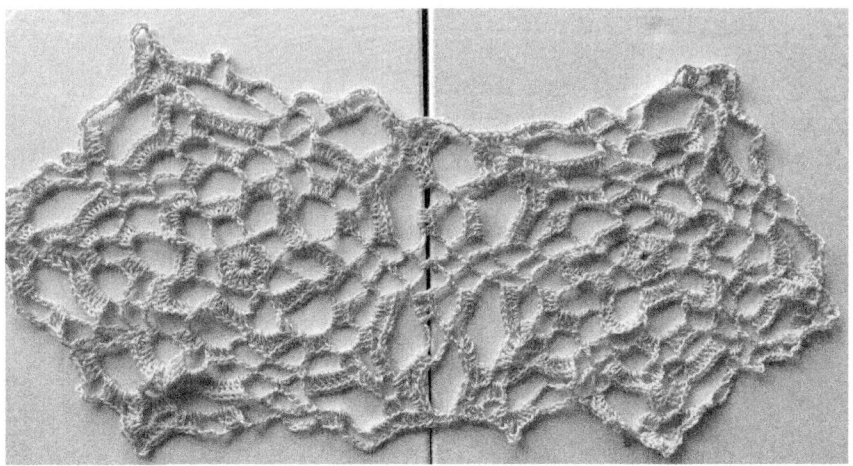

Photo 22: Motif 2 joined to Motif 1 along shared edge.

Motif 3: Referring back to Figure 1, you'll see that Motif 3 will join to Motif 2 along Motif 2's side edge. All other edges of Motif 3 will be completed as 'unjoined' edges.

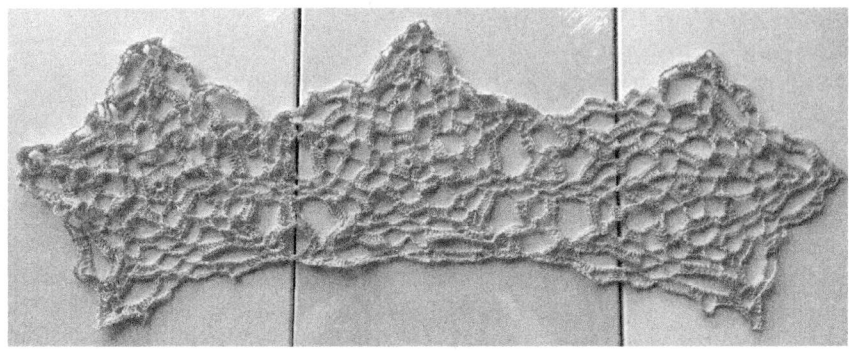

Photo 23: Garment after first three joined motifs.

Motif 4: Motif 4 joins on one side to Motif 1. The remaining edges of Motif 4 are completed as unjoined edges. The other edges will eventually join to other motifs as we progress through the pattern.

Motif 5 joins on three of its five edges. Begin by joining to the side edge of Motif 4, then join to top edge of Motif 1 and then to Motif 2. The last two edges are completed as unjoined edges.

Motif 6: Motif 6 joins on two of its five sides. Join first to Motif 2 and then to Motif 3. Notice that Motif 6 does **not** join to Motif 5 because this edge is left open for the lower half of the back-opening.

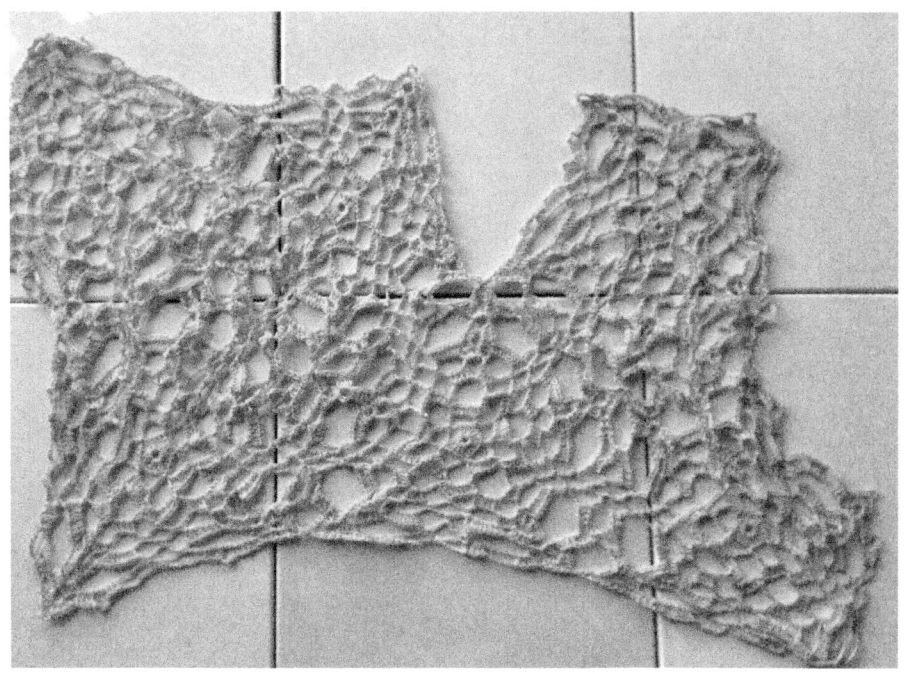

Photo 24: The first 6 joined pentagonal motifs.

Motif 7: Motif 7 joins on two of its five sides. Join first to Motif 6 and then to Motif 3. The other sides are completed as unjoined sides. They will eventually be joined when we add the square motifs (11 & 13).

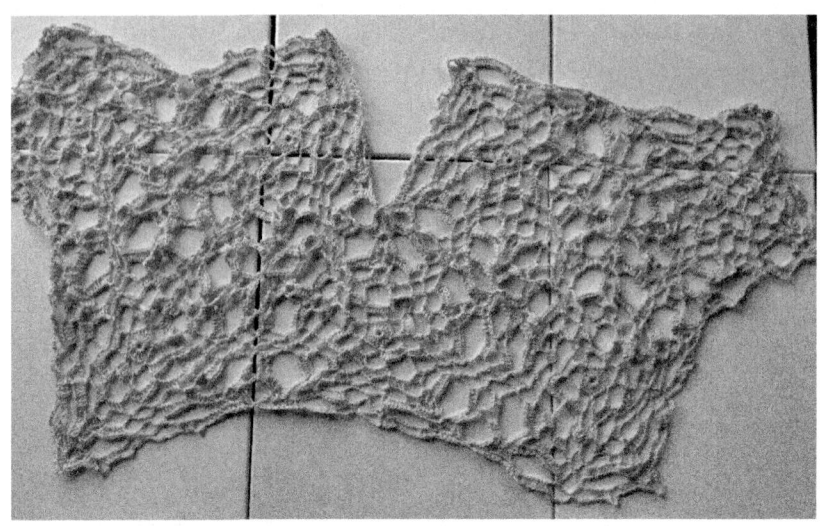

Photo 25: The first 7 joined pentagonal motifs

The Square Motif Pattern

Motifs 8-13

Motifs 8-13 are square motifs. The pattern for the square motifs is nearly identical to the pentagonal pattern except that we need to adjust the first two rounds to allow for a multiple of four rather than five. This will allow us to create a four-sided rather than five-sided motif.

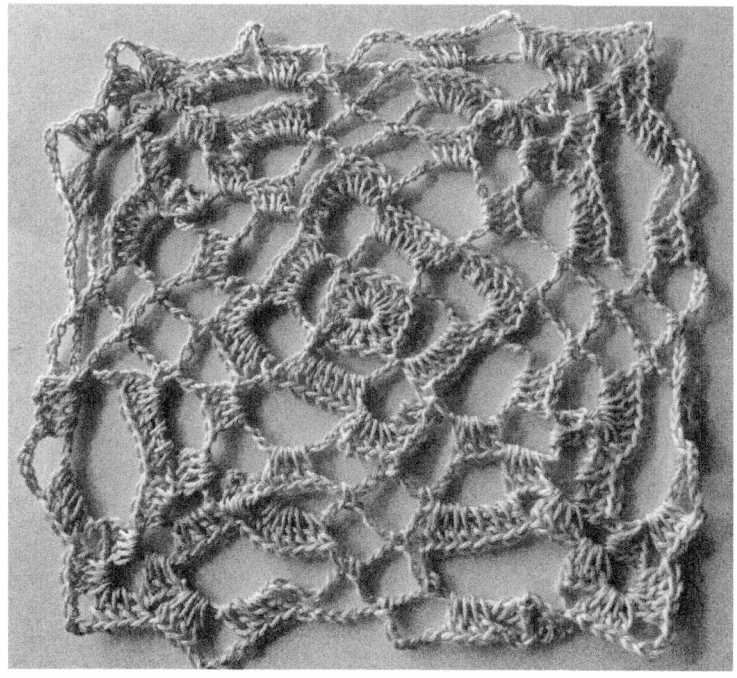

Photo 26: The completed Square Motif

To create the square motifs begin with:

Ch4. Slip stitch in first stitch of starting chain to form a ring.

Round 1 (Rd 1): ch3 (acts as 1st dc); 15dc in ring. Slip stitch to top of opening ch3 to end the round.

End with 16 dc.

Rd2-Rd9: Repeat Rd2-Rd9 of the Pentagon Pattern. At the end of each round the number of chain spaces or loops will be a multiple of 4 rather than 5.

Joining Motifs 8-13

Motif 8: Square Motif 8 joins to Pentagon Motif 4 along Motif 4's top edge. The remaining three edges of Motif 8 are completed as unjoined edges.

Motif 9: Looking at Figure 1, notice that Motif 9 joins to Square Motif 8 and Pentagon Motif 5. Once you have completed these two consecutive shared edges, complete the last two edges of Motif 9 as 'unjoined' edges.

Motif 10: Motif 10 is a "special join". Notice in Figure 1, that Motif 10 joins to Motif 9 only in one corner. Motif 10 then joins to Pentagon Motif 6 along Motif 6's top edge. The join in the corner will create the halter neck portion of the garment and the unjoined edges of Motifs 9 and 10 will create the upper half of the halter back of the cascading cardigan.

Motif 11: Motif 11 joins first to Motif 10 and then to the top edge of Pentagon Motif 7. The remaining two edges of Motif 11 are completed as unjoined edges.

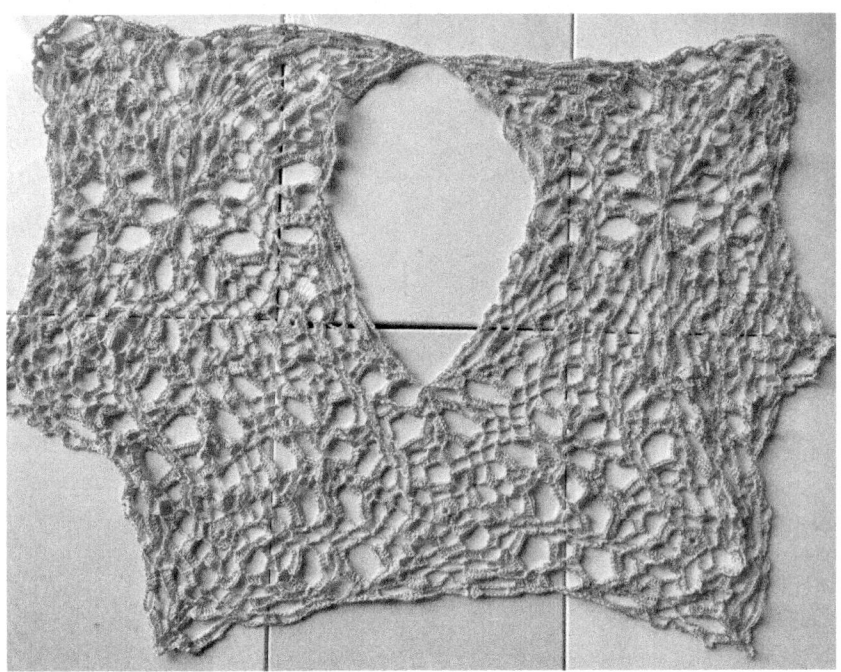

Photo 27: The garment after joining Motifs 1-11.

46

All that remains is to complete two more square motifs in the lower corners of the garment. These are Motifs 12 & 13 in Figure 1.

Motif 12 joins first to Pentagon Motif 1 along Motif 1's left side and then to Motif 4 along Motif 4's bottom edge. The remaining two edges are finished as unjoined edges.

Finally, **Motif 13** joins first to Pentagon Motif 7 along Motif 7's bottom edge and then to Motif 3 along Motif 3's right side edge. The remaining two edges are finished as unjoined edges.

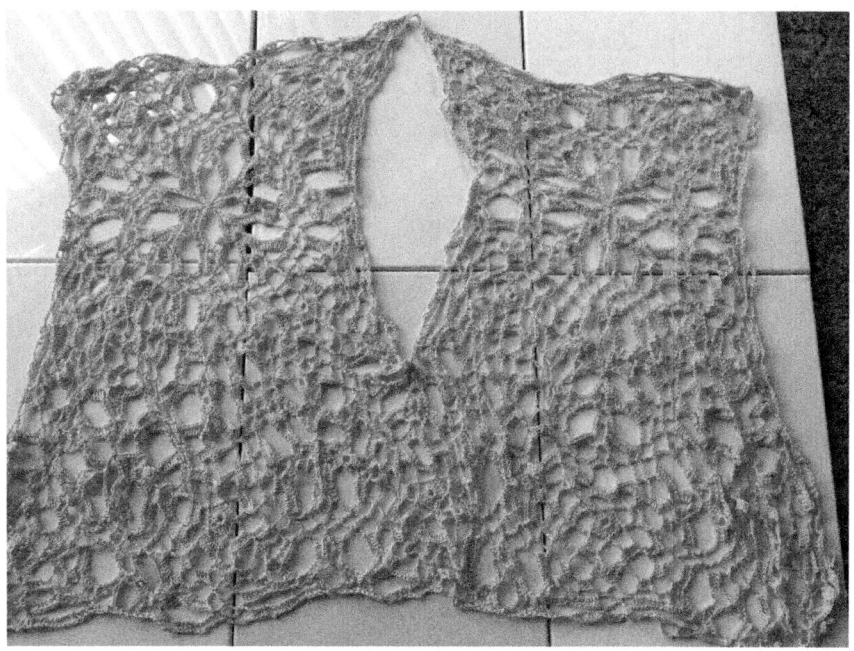

Photo 28: The garment after joining all Motifs 1-13.

After you successfully join Motif 13, you have finished the motif portion of the pattern. Congratulations! Your garment is nearly complete. All that remains is to add trim to the back-opening and perimeter edge and then block the garment.

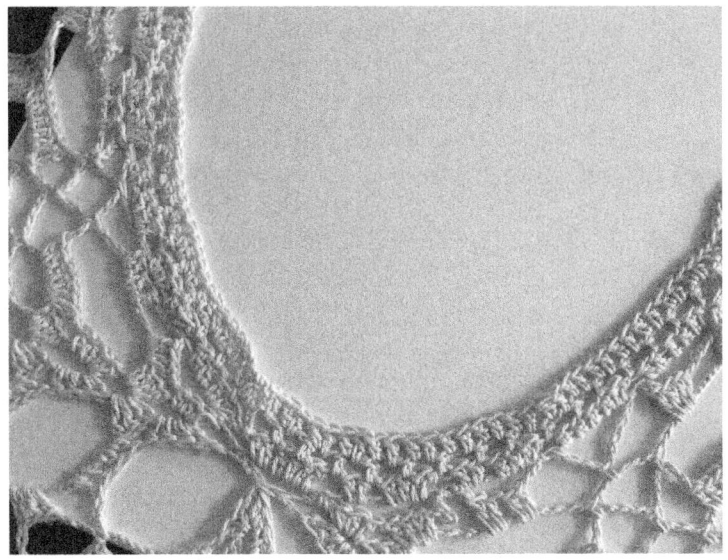

Photo 29: Back-Opening Trim.

Trim

The trim for the back-opening and the perimeter will use similar stitches. We will, however, be binding the back-opening a little tighter than we will the perimeter edging.

Edging for Back-Opening

We will now add a decorative trim to the back-opening.

Joining the yarn: We will start by making a round of ch8 loops. Begin by joining the yarn on the right side of the garment in the ch4 corner space where the motifs join in the bottom center of the back.

Back-Opening Trim Rd1: *ch8; sc in next available chain space (either a ch6 side loop or a ch4 corner loop**; repeat from * to ** around all four motifs that make up the back-opening.

You should end with 24 ch8 loops.

Back-Opening Trim Rd2: Work 8dc into each ch8 loop. Slip stitch to top of first dc to end the round.

(**Designer Note**: At this point, try the garment on by putting both arms through the back-opening so that the cardigan wraps around your neck and back and cascades down the front. For a looser fitting garment, change Rd1 to ch10 loops and then work 10dc into each loop in Rd2. For a tighter fitting garment, change Rd1 to a ch6 loop and work 6dc into each loop in Round 2.)

Back-Opening Trim Rd3: ch4 (acts as the first dc plus a ch1); *skip 1 dc; dc in next dc; ch1**; repeat from * to ** around. Slip stitch to third chain stitch to end the round. (Basically a round of (ch1, dc) in every other dc around.)

Back-Opening Trim Rd4: ch3 (acts as first dc), dc in each ch1 space and dc in each dc around the entire back-opening. Slip stitch to the top of the opening ch3 to end the round. (Basically a round of all dc.)

Fasten off. Weave in ends. Proceed to perimeter edging.

Cascading Cardigan Vest Lace Crochet Pattern

Photo 30: Back view of completed garment.

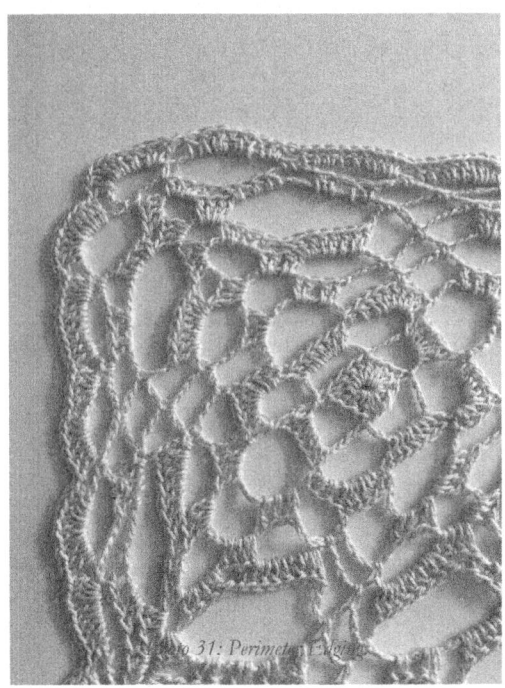

Photo 31: Perimeter Edging

Simple Perimeter Edging.

We will begin by making a round of ch10 loops around the entire perimeter with an extra "loop" in each of the four corners to accentuate the corner of the garment

Joining the yarn: Join the yarn on the right side of the garment in the corner ch4 space where Motif 9 joins to Motif 10 at the top back center of garment.

Perimeter Edging Rd1: *[ch10; sc in next ch6 space]**4 times**; ch10**; sc in next ch4 corner space; ch10; sc in ch4 corner space of next motif***. Repeat from * to ** one more time to reach the outer left corner of Motif 8. Work (sc, ch10, sc) in the outer ch4 corner space of Motif 8. (**Note:** This extra loop in the corner allows us to give a nice curve the edge of the garment when we complete the perimeter edging.) Repeat from * to *** until you reach the outer corner of Motif 12 at the bottom of the garment. Work (sc, ch10, sc) in the outer corner ch4 space of Motif 12. Repeat * to *** along bottom edge of garment until you reach the outer corner ch4 space of Motif 13. Work (sc, ch10, sc) in the outer corner ch4 of Motif 13. Repeat * to *** along side edge until you reach the outer ch4 corner space of Motif 11 at top right corner. Work (sc, ch10, sc) in the outer ch4 corner space of Motif 11. Repeat * to *** until you return to center back.

You should have 90 ch10 loops around perimeter.

Perimeter Edging Rd2: Work 10dc in each ch10 space around entire perimeter. Slip stitch to top of first dc to end the round.

You've finished the simple trim of the garment! All that remains is to stretch and block the garment to your desired dimensions.

Photo 32: Completed garment after edging.

Finishing Touches & Blocking

This garment definitely requires shaping and blocking to achieve the right fit and dimensions. You will want to gently shape the garment to smooth out the motif edges especially around the joining stitches. You want the edges to seamlessly blend into one another and look like lacework rather than appear as a collection of identifiable shapes. You will notice that the garment gets longer and wider as you gently shape the motifs, especially near the joining stitches. Be careful not to overstretch the garment while smoothing out the corner joins. The design of the garment will stretch as you wear it.

Blocking is very important. This will smooth out the motif joins and give a nice polished look to your joining edges. Wet the garment, gently wring out the excess moisture and lay it onto a towel. Shape the garment into the desired dimensions, or use my dimensions as a guideline. Place another towel over the wet garment. Lay flat to dry. Once dry, enjoy your new garment!

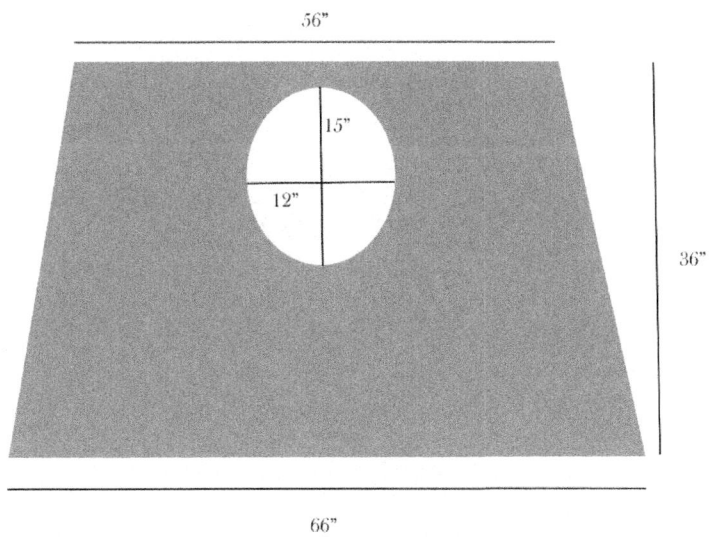

Photo 33: Suggested Dimensions of finished garment when blocking.

Photo 34: Completed Garment Front.

Photo 35: Side view

Photo 36: Back View

Concluding Remarks

Congratulations on completing your "Cascading Cardigan Vest". I hope you agree that lace motif crochet is a beautiful, fast, fun and exciting way to design garments. The pieces are feminine, romantic & delicate. They have a fluidity to them that shape gently across the body and are flattering on all body types. I hope you are pleased with the item that you created and that you enjoyed making the motif garment as much as I enjoyed designing it. If you were pleased with the book, and the pattern in particular, please leave a review. If you discover any errors, or have any questions, please write to me through my author's bookpage, or through my blog at http://kristensteinfineart.blogspot.com.

I look forward to hearing from you. Please take a look at my other recent pattern books and designing sketchbooks (digital and paperback). I have many other patterns available as shown on the next page.

Other Recent Pattern Books

Most recently added:

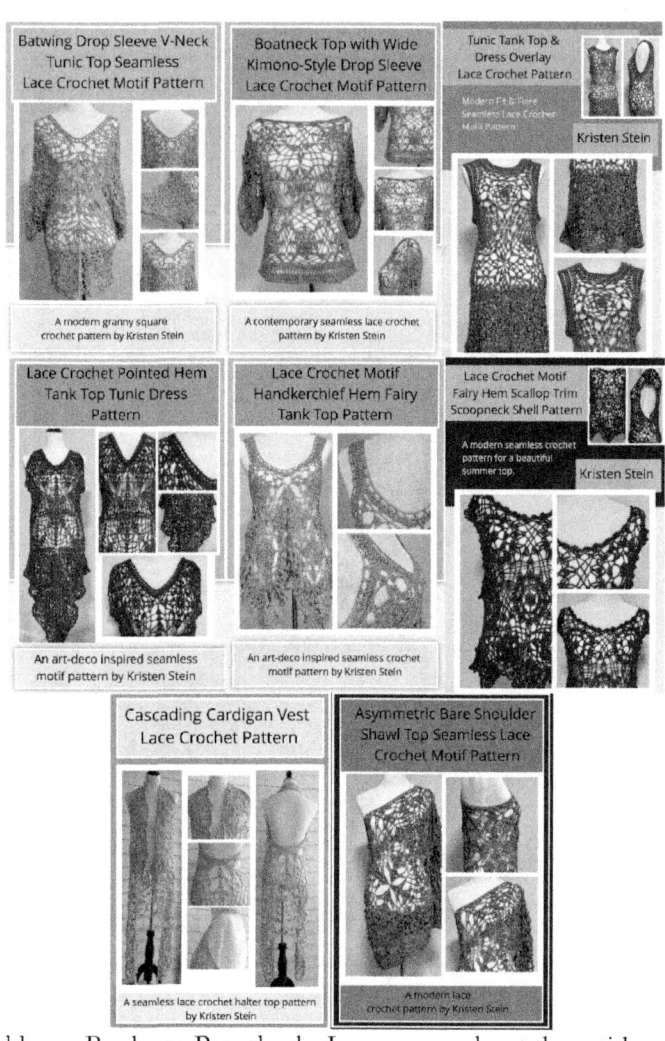

Available as eBooks or Paperbacks Learn more about these titles on my
blog: http://kristensteinfineart.blogspot.com
or search Amazon for Kristen Stein.

Additional sketch and design books are also available. Visit my Amazon author page or blog for more information.

Photo 38: New line of sketch & design books.

New line of sketchbook and design books to aid in the design process for fashion designers, especially those that knit, crochet, sew or quilt. The designer's notebooks have both lined and patterned pages to provide an area to sketch out the design and an area to write pattern notes.

Stitch Glossary

Chain stitch (ch) - Start with a slipknot. Insert your crochet hook through the slipknot then pick up the yarn with the hook. Pull the yarn through the slip knot back to front. This is the first chain stitch.

Double-crochet (dc) - Yarn over the hook, insert hook into the next stitch to be worked and yarn over again. Pull the yarn through the stitch and yarn over again. You should now have three loops on the hook. Pull the yarn through both loops and yarn over again. Pull yarn through the last two loops on the hook to complete the double crochet.

Half-Double-Crochet (hdc) – Similar to a double-crochet, but it ends up with a slightly shorter stitch. Yarn over the hook, insert hook into the next stitch to be worked and yarn over again. Pull the yarn through the stitch and yarn over again. You should now have three loops on the hook. Pull the yarn all three loops to complete the half-double crochet.

Picot (p) – The picot is a decorative stitch that is often used in borders or trim to add a little extra charm or flourish to the final project. The most common picot is the ch3 or ch4 picot. My patterns use the ch3 picot (unless otherwise noted). To create a ch3 picot, simply ch3 and then insert your hook in the third chain from hook. Yarn over and pull through the stitch and through the loop on the hook . Basically, you ch3 and then slip stitch into the first chain of the ch3. This will create a tight little "dot" that adds a nice decorative trim to the final piece.

Single Crochet (sc) - Insert the hook into stitch. Yarnover and pull the yarn through the loop on your hook. Yarn over again and pull the yarn through both loops on your hook. You've created one single crochet stitch.

Slip stitch (sl st) - Slip stitches are convenient for transitioning between rounds and helping to move the yarn or thread to different starting positions without adding height or bulk. To make a slip stitch, insert your hook through the desired space. Hook your yarn and pull it through. You've just made your first slip stitch.

Treble crochet (tr) - Also called a triple crochet. Yarn over your hook twice. Insert the hook into the next stitch. Yarn over and draw the yarn through the stitch. You should have four loops on the hook. Yarn over the hook again and draw the yarn through two of the four loops on the hook. Yarn over again and draw through two more loops. Yarn over again and draw through last two loops. You should be left with one loop on hook to start next stitch.

Treble-crochet-together (trtog) – This stitch creates a cluster of treble crochets all sharing the same stitch space. *Yarn over twice, insert your hook into stitch, yarn over and pull up a loop. Yarn over and draw through 2 loops. Yarn over and draw through two loops again. Yarn over twice, insert hook in same stitch, yarn over and pull up a loop, yarn over and draw through two loops, yarn over and draw through 2 loops (you should now have 3 loops on hook.) **

For a **tr2tog**, yarn over and draw through the last 3 loops on the hook to complete the tr2tog.

For a **tr3tog,** do * to ** as described above, but to create the third trtog, you will need to yarn over twice, insert the hook into the same stitch again and then yarn over and draw up a loop, yarn over and draw through 2 loops, yarn over and draw through 2 more loops, (you'll have 4 loops on the hook), yarn over and draw through all 4 loops on the hook. You have now created a **tr3tog cluster**.

About the Artist & Designer

Kristen Stein is an award-winning Contemporary Artist living in Suburban Philadelphia. Kristen's works are currently available on a variety of online venues and boutiques and galleries throughout the US. Her art has appeared in numerous printed media including posters, books, CD Covers, calendars and program covers. Her work has been licensed for use on gift items, household goods, puzzles and jewelry items. Her work has appeared in a number of solo and group exhibitions and in the set design for various television shows and a major motion picture. Although the bulk of her portfolio focuses on her original paintings and designs, Kristen also enjoys needlework and creating her own original crochet patterns. A self-proclaimed "espresso aficionado", Kristen is still trying to master the latte art technique. Although, nowhere near perfecting the technique, she still enjoys every delicious attempt.

Please visit http://kristensteinfineart.blogspot.com or http://StudioArtworks.com for more information.

Printed in Dunstable, United Kingdom

71823347R00040